EASTER DAFFO[DILS]

EASTER EGG AND DAFFODIL CLIP ART FOR HANDMADE CARDS, [...]
EASY PRE-PRINTED PAPER CRAFTS TO CUT, GLUE A[...]

The Anni Arts printable crafts are now in this easy and ready-[...] ormat.
'Print-on-demand' makes printing as environmentally friendly as printi[n]g [t]he crafts at home.

PROJECTS

SEE THE EQUIPMENT GUIDE, TIPS AND GENERAL INSTRUCTIONS ON THE FOLLOWING PAGE
SEE CARD KIT AND CUP CARD INSTRUCTIONS PLUS CHOC WRAPPER TIPS ON THE LAST TWO PAGES
ALL PAGES HAVE THE RELEVANT INSTRUCTIONS PRINTED WITH THE PAPER CRAFT ITEM.

GREETING CARDS

SHAPED STAND-UP TEACUP CRADLE CARD WITH BACK STAND – on front and back covers
TWO-PART ENVELOPE FOR CUP CARD – with pretty dotty inner lining
TEA BAG PACKET TO ADD TO THE TEACUP CARD AS A LITTLE FAVOUR
5" x 7" DECOUPAGE CARD WITH LAYERS
TWO-PART ENVELOPE FOR THE 5" x 7" LAYER CARD – with pretty dotty inner lining
TOPPER WITH EASTER WISHES AND EGGS FOR A 4" x 6" POSTCARD OR A CARD THAT FOLDS TO 4"x6"
Download free blank templates for a 4"x6" and 5" x 7"card to print

PAPER CRAFTS AND PACKS

EASTER EGG WRAPS FOR SMALL EGGS – these can also be used as serviette rings
CUPCAKE WRAPS AND TOPPERS – *Download additional printable cupcake wrappers in the freebie file*
GIFT BAG FOR A GIFT, CHOCOLATES OR SMALL EASTER EGGS – use with included handles or ribbon
TEA TOTE – A GIFT TOTE FILLED WITH TEABAGS IN ENVELOPES – add ribbon handles
LARGE CHOCOLATE WRAPPER FOR A CHOCOLATE SLAB
SMALL CHOCOLATE WRAPPER FOR A SNACK CHOCOLATE OR HERSHEY BAR
GIFT TAG ASSORTMENT – on the covers
ASSORTED LABELS, ENVELOPE SEALS AND SENTIMENT STRIPS – plus extra bits to use with the paper crafts

DÉCOR

3D EGG-SHAPED EASTER DECORATIONS
EASTER FLAGS – E-A-S-T-E-R BUNTING to use as décor
A SMALL BOWL OR *BONBONNIERE* FOR LITTLE EGG CHOCOLATES OR TRUFFLES

ALSO SEE *Easter Daffodils Printable Crafts with Easter themes as downloads or on craft CD/ USB.*
With Cards, 3D Cups and Saucers and more. From ANNI ARTS CRAFTS *at* **www.anniartscrafts.com**
The Anni Arts Easter Daffodils are also on fun, ready-to-buy products like mugs, chocolate boxes and cakes.

READY TO BUY

Chocolate Cocoa Mix

PRINTABLES

ANNI ARTS

FREE EXTRAS *Download additional items to print at:* ANNI ARTS www.anniarts.com/daffodil-clip-art

EQUIPMENT

SCISSORS small and sharp for detail and large for cutting the craft pages from the book
CRAFT KNIFE with a sharp blade to cut straight lines (optional)
RULER with a metal edge if used with a craft knife
GLUE STICK
ADHESIVE TAPE as an alternative to glue on some items. Double-sided tape is best, as it can be concealed.
PAPER SCORER
A paper scorer is an instrument to draw a line to make folding that line easier.
It makes a dent on the card or paper, but does not cut right through. It is essential for creating tidy and precise paper crafts. Craft shops sell special scoring instruments, but an empty ballpoint pen is just as efficient - and is my personal favorite! You can also use the blunt side of the blade of a craft knife to make a *very light* score. And in a pinch you can also use a butter knife (with no serrations on the blade).
Note: When scoring regular paper like that on **the pages in this Cut-N-Make book**, take care to *score lightly* – the paper can easily tear if the score runs too deep. However, items on the **covers** *do need deep scores*.

TIPS AND GENERAL INSTRUCTIONS

All pages have the relevant instructions printed with the paper craft item. Also see the specific instructions for the cup card, decoupage card and egg decorations, as well as ideas for the chocolate wrappers and card layouts on the last two pages.

TIPS:

First cut each craft page from the book along the guide line.
Then score all lines as indicated.
Cut out the shape of the pre-printed card element or craft template.
Fold on the scored lines and glue as indicated.
Add labels, seals and tags as desired.

GREETING CARDS:

Make sure that glue goes all the way to the edges of the card elements. Lay a blank piece of paper over a freshly positioned and glued element and glide the edge of a ruler over the covered section to flatten and properly glue the element to the underlying layer. The cover paper protects the glued elements.

The elements for the 5"x7" card are for layering in sequential decoupage layers – starting with the dotty patch used as a backing layer. The layers give a nice embossed, decoupage look. *The paper elements are NOT suitable for dimensional lifting by layering over foam squares. (If dimensional layering is desired, first glue the kit elements to cardstock and then proceed with the card layout.)*

The *card and the postcard* need to be constructed from *cardstock*, as the paper in this book is not heavy enough for a card base. The backing patch of the decoupage card is glued to a blank card cut from cardstock. Cut card bases to the dimensions given below, or *download the printable blank templates and print* the card bases on printable cardstock from Anni Arts at www.anniarts.com/daffodil-clip-art

*Cut a **10" x 7" (approx. 25.5 x17.75 cm)** backing for a card that folds to **5"x 7"**. Or cut 5" x 7" for a postcard.*
*Cut a **8" x 6" (approx. 20 x 15 cm)** backing for a card that folds to **4" x 6"**. Or cut 4" x 6" for a postcard.*
Score through the middle to fold the card and add the cardmaking elements to the front.

SEE THE GROWING LIST OF ANNI ARTS CUT-N-MAKE BOOK TITLES – CHECK www.anniarts.com FOR UPDATES!

ANNI ARTS
CUT-N-MAKE
BOOKS

TULIPS & EASTER EGGS
REINDEER TOILE DE JOUY
SCANDINAVIAN CHRISTMAS

DAFFODILS and EGG LAYER CARD

cut around egg and
flower shapes

cut bottom line
straight on either side of
egg shape

Layer Elements

The other card elements
* are on the page
with the back
section of the
envelope

See the
instructions
on the last
two pages

Base of layer card

Extra border element

Fold side and bottom tabs back after scoring and glue to envelope back so that back patch is on top of the folded and glued tabs

-score

-score

-score

-score

ANNI ARTS

Extra border element

* * * *

Optional envelope seal

LAYER CARD
ELEMENTS

EASTER
GREETINGS

HAPPY
EASTER

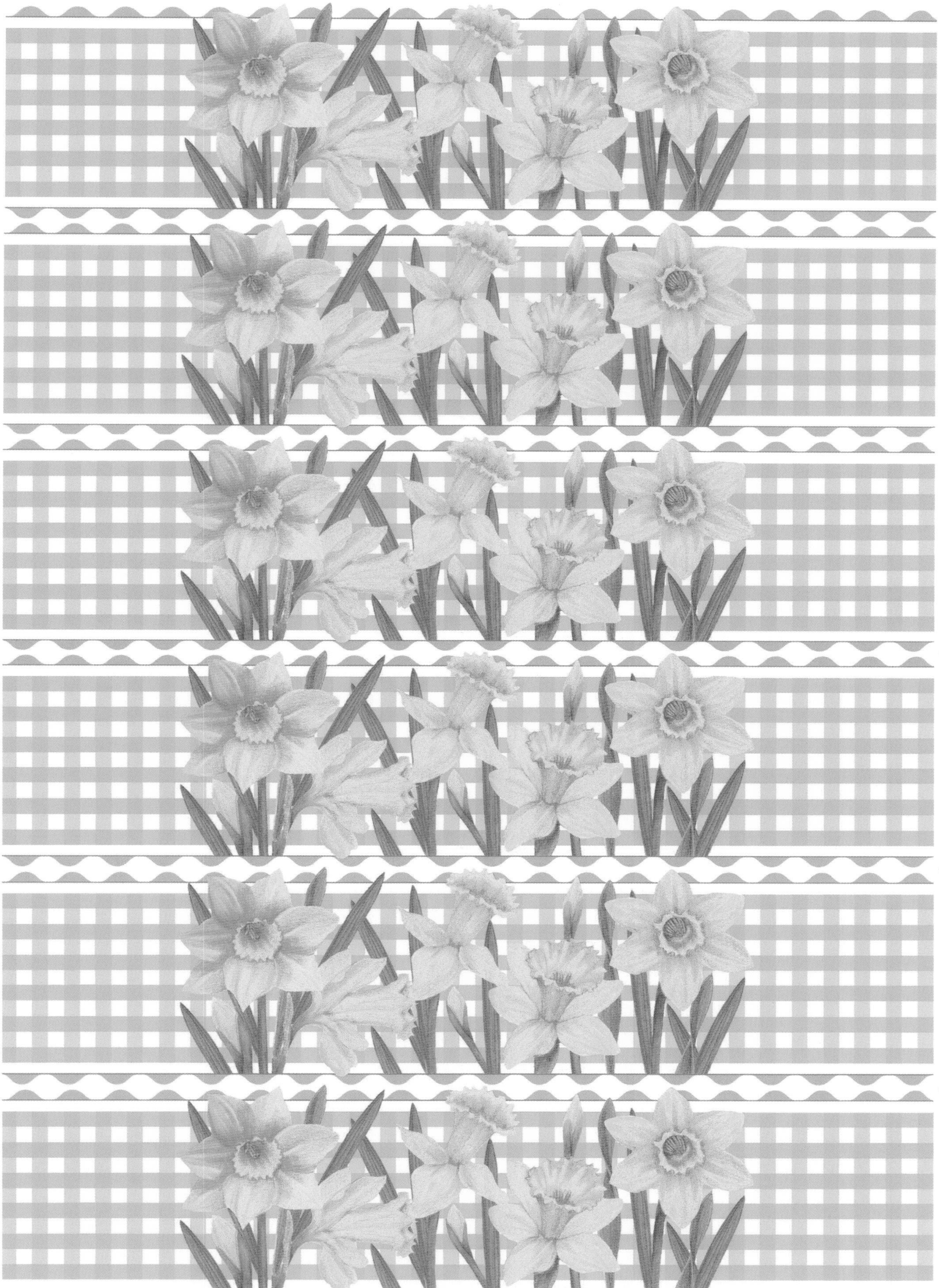

EGG STANDS FOR SMALL EGGS OR SERVIETTE RINGS
Trim as needed

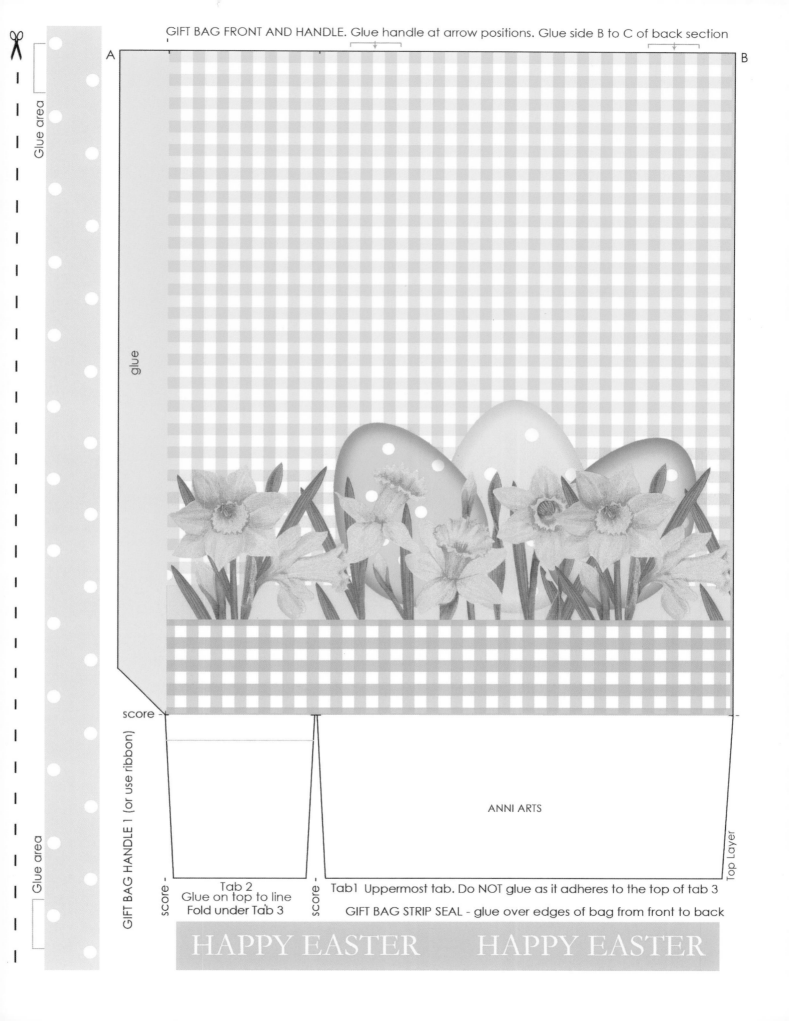

GIFT BAG FRONT AND HANDLE. Glue handle at arrow positions. Glue side B to C of back section

A   B

Glue area

Glue area

glue

score

score

score

GIFT BAG HANDLE 1 (or use ribbon)

Tab 2
Glue on top to line
Fold under Tab 3

Tab1 Uppermost tab. Do NOT glue as it adheres to the top of tab 3

GIFT BAG STRIP SEAL - glue over edges of bag from front to back

ANNI ARTS

Top Layer

HAPPY EASTER   HAPPY EASTER

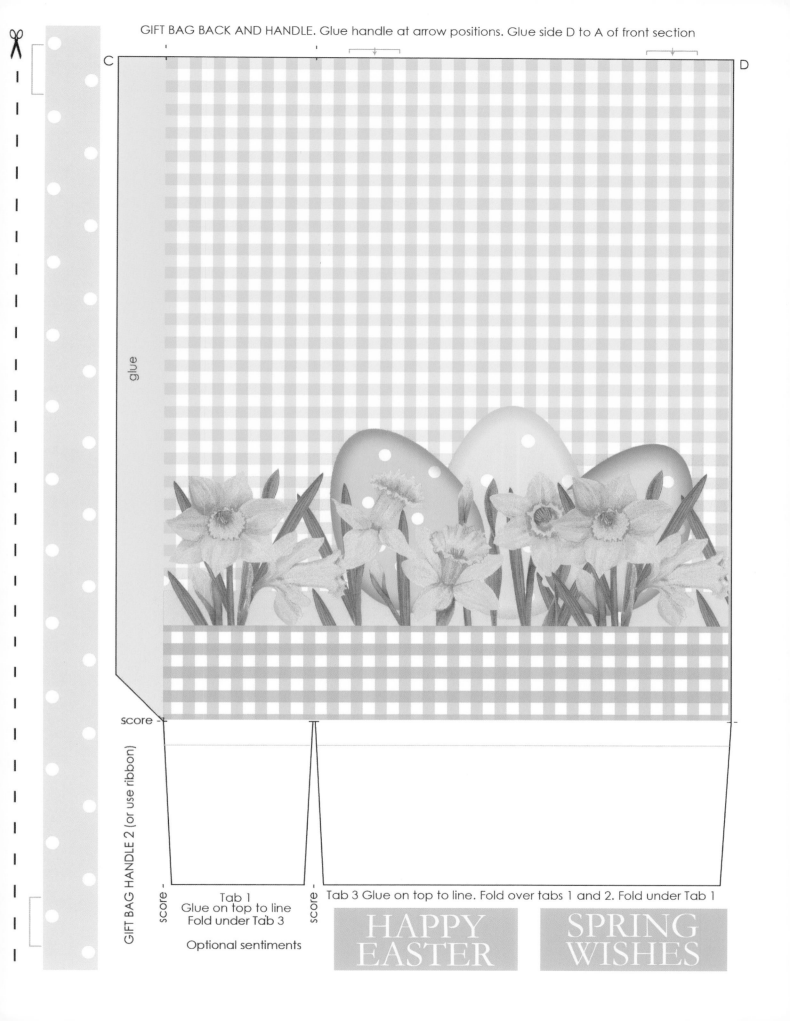

GIFT BAG BACK AND HANDLE. Glue handle at arrow positions. Glue side D to A of front section

C

D

glue

score

GIFT BAG HANDLE 2 (or use ribbon)

score

Tab 1
Glue on top to line
Fold under Tab 3

Optional sentiments

score

Tab 3 Glue on top to line. Fold over tabs 1 and 2. Fold under Tab 1

HAPPY EASTER

SPRING WISHES

Reinforcement tab. Score, glue on under side and fold in. Flatten and glue sedurely. Let glue dry.Punch holes on grey dots. Thread ribbon

ANNI ARTS

Cut just
inside the
outline

ANNI ARTS

Cut just
inside the
outline

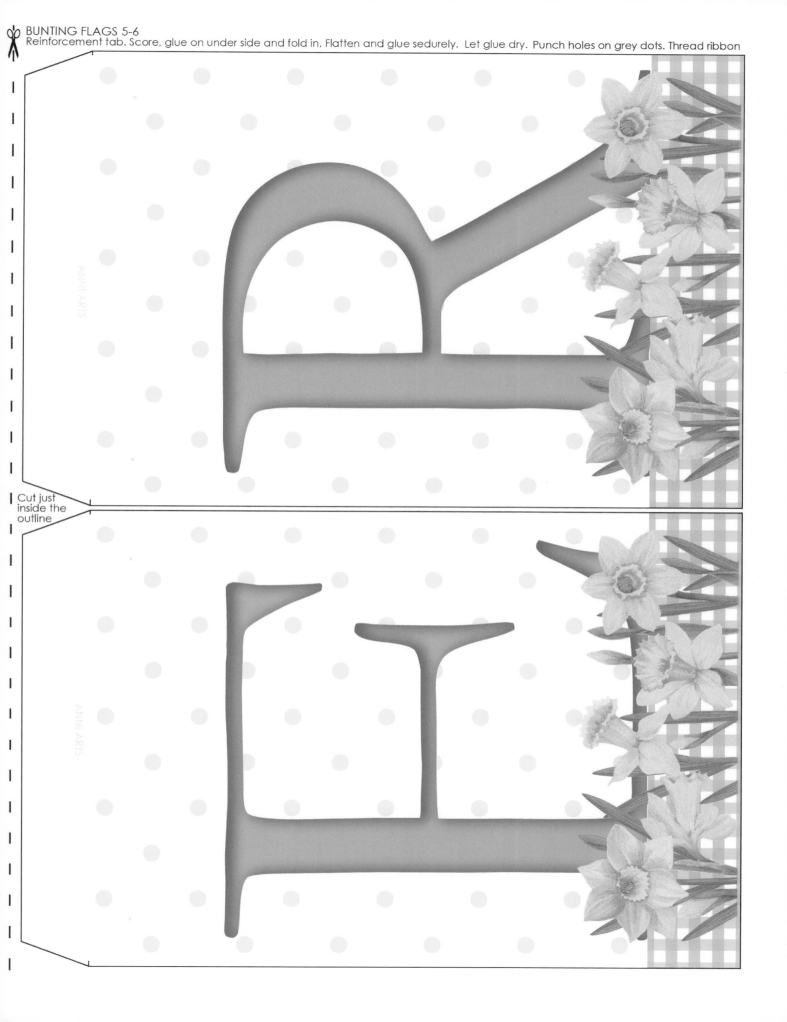

Cut just
inside the
outline

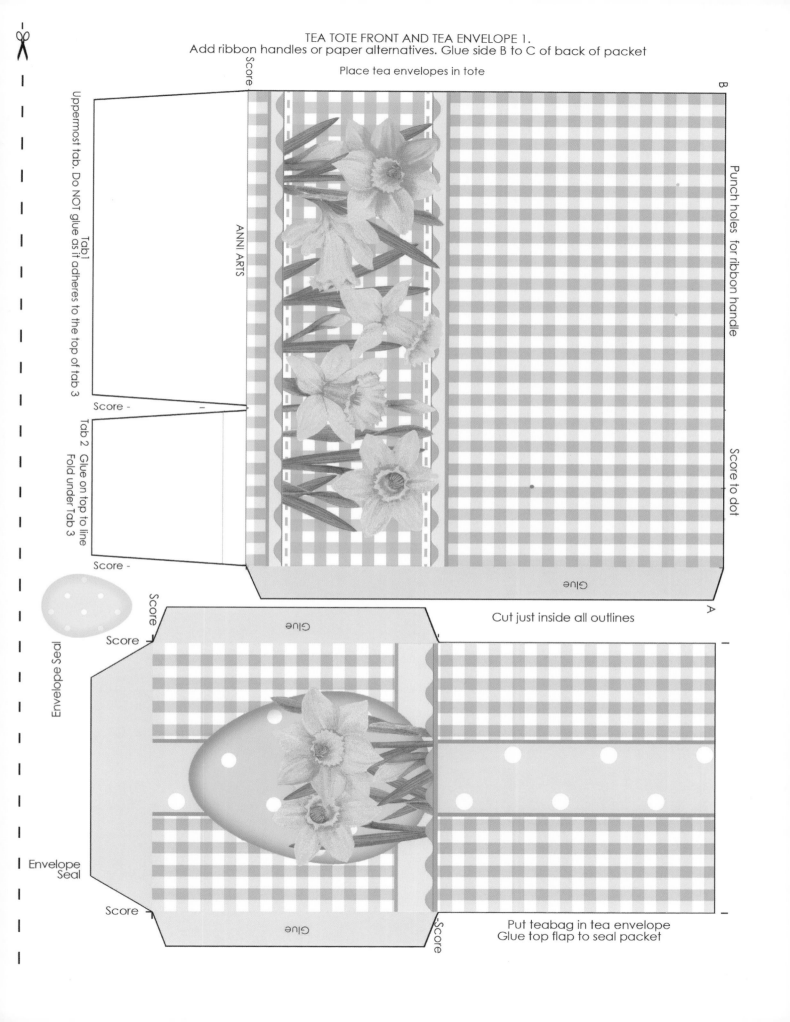

TEA TOTE FRONT AND TEA ENVELOPE 1.
Add ribbon handles or paper alternatives. Glue side B to C of back of packet

Place tea envelopes in tote

Tab 1
Uppermost tab. Do NOT glue as it adheres to the top of tab 3

Score -   –

Tab 2   Glue on top to line
Fold under Tab 3

Score -

Score -

ANNI ARTS

Score

B

Punch holes for ribbon handle

Score to dot

Glue

A

Cut just inside all outlines

Envelope Seal

Envelope
Seal

Score

Score

Score

Glue

Glue

Glue

Score

Put teabag in tea envelope
Glue top flap to seal packet

TEA TOTE BACK AND TEA ENVELOPE 2.
Add ribbon handles or paper alternatives. Glue side D to A of front of packet
Punch holes for a ribbon handle and add a tag.

D

Punch holes for ribbon handle

Score to dot

Score

Tab 3
Glue on top to line

Score -

Tab 2   Glue on top to line
Fold under Tab 3

Score -

Glue

Cut just inside all outlines

C

Score
Score

Glue

Score
Score

Glue

Score

Put teabag in tea envelope
Glue top flap to seal packet

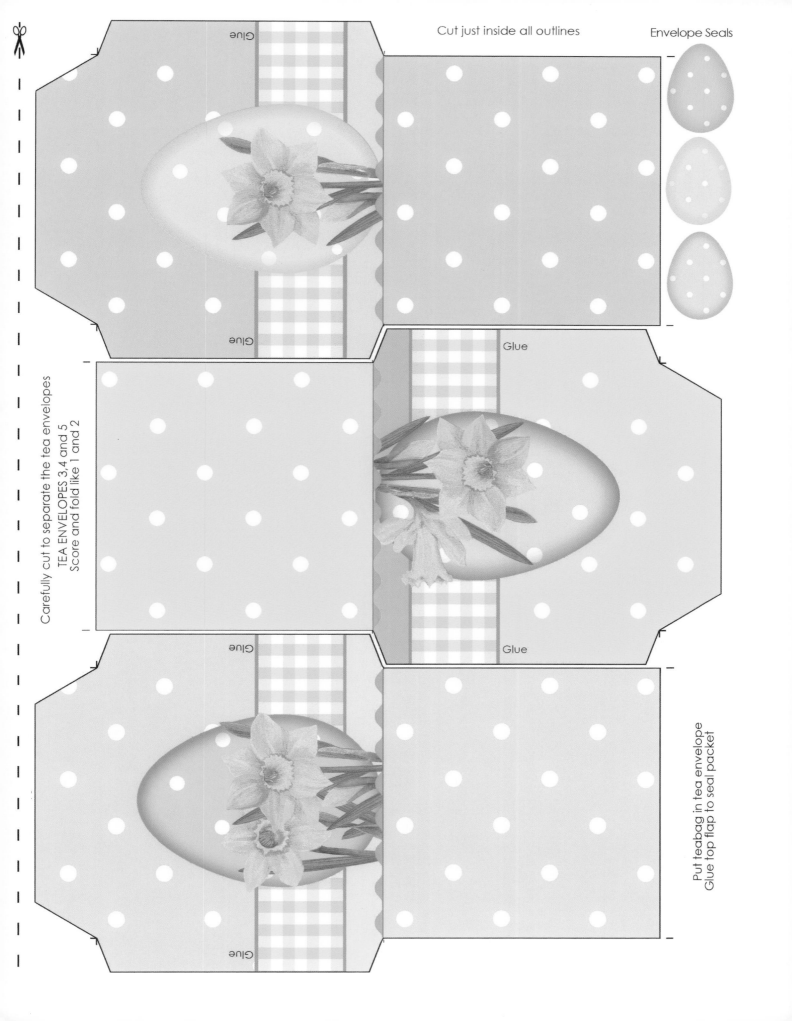

Glue

Glue

Cut just inside all outlines

Envelope Seals

Glue

Glue

Glue

Carefully cut to separate the tea envelopes
TEA ENVELOPES 3,4 and 5
Score and fold like 1 and 2

Glue

Glue

Put teabag in tea envelope
Glue top flap to seal packet

CUPCAKE WRAPPERS
TOPPERS and
FLAGS

Score topper
line, cut egg
shape, fold
and glue over
a toothpick

HAPPY EASTER

Score and fold here.

Extra elements

SPRING WISHES

SPRING WISHES

Score and fold here.

HAPPY EASTER

Tape or glue the
wrapper around
a cupcake

Download additional
cupcake wrappers and
print as many as needed at
ANNI ARTS
www.anniarts.com/daffodil-clip-art

SLEEVE FOR SMALL SNACK CHOC LIKE HERSHEY OR CADBURY

Glue and seal back seam of wrapper sleeve. Place choccie inside.
Flatten edges. Glue each edge on inside by placing tip of
glue stick inside sleeve. Flatten for a flat edge with a "crimped" look.
The edges can also be cut with decorative scissors.
Alternatively, first wrap the chocolate in tissue paper.
Trim the wrapper and wrap over the tissue paper.
so that the tissue edges show

HAPPY EASTER

4"x 6" POSTCARD OR CARD TOPPER

Score   Alternative trim edge

Score

Score

Alternative trim edge   Score

ANNI ARTS

TWO-PART ENVELOPE FRONT FOR TEACUP CRADLE CARD

Optional address label

Stamps, for hand-delivered greeting cards

Score and fold

Fold side and bottom tabs back after scoring and glue to envelope back so that back patch is on top of the folded and glued tabs

The following page forms the lining of the envelope and backet

Score and fold

FOR 5" x 7" OR 12.5 x 17.75 cm CARD

Score

Score

✂

Extra element

First cut on grey outlines. Score, glue and fold over teabag string. The following page forms the lining of the envelope and packet Cut egg shape when glue is dry

HAPPY
EASTER

HAPPY
EASTER

TWO-PART ENVELOPE BACK FOR TEACUP CRADLE CARD

Glue top
tabs after
tea bag
has been
placed in
the packet

Glue —

Glue —

Score

Score

Glue —

Punch –
hole for
tea bag
string

Glue —

TEA BAG FAVOUR FOR
STAND-UP TEACUP CARD

Score —

Score lines on packet
and fold.

Score
lines

Glue side and bottom
tabs to make a packet.

Place a teabag, with its
string and tag, in the
packet and glue and
close the top tabs.

TIP: Shake the tea
leaves in the tea bag
to distribute them
evenly before placing
it in the packet.

Replace the tag
attached to the tea
bag with the egg tag
The egg tag dangles
on the front of the
teacup card.

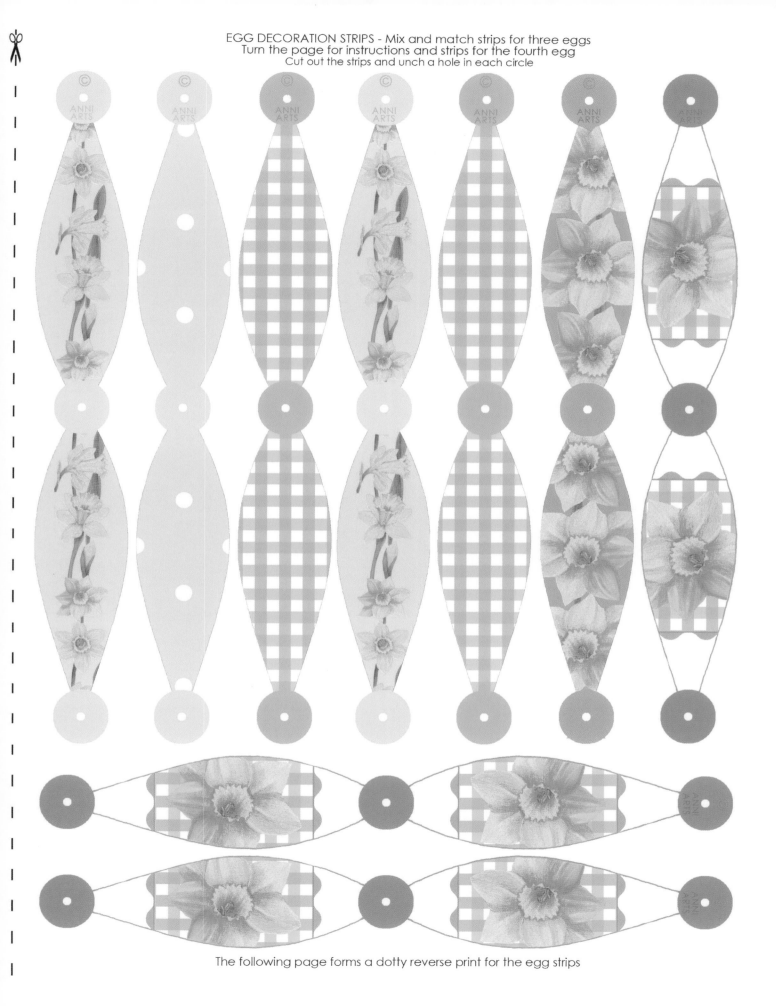

EGG DECORATION STRIPS - Mix and match strips for three eggs
Turn the page for instructions and strips for the fourth egg
Cut out the strips and unch a hole in each circle

The following page forms a dotty reverse print for the egg strips

EGG DECORATION INSTRUCTIONS

1. You will need a hole punch and about 20 inches/50 cm of ribbon for each hanging egg.

The wider the ribbon, the bigger the size of the knots - which help to keep the nice egg shape of the finished egg.

Mix and match the patterns for all the eggs - but at least one can be made up all in the same pattern. There are enough strips for four eggs.

2. Cut out all the strips. Three lengths are needed for each egg. One by one, punch holes through the end circles and centre of each strip.

3. Lay out the strips with their centres layered together.

4. Thread the start of a ribbon through the centre leaving a tail. The pattern must face up.

5. Tie a knot to keep the centres from slipping through. The knot must be bigger than the hole.

6. Measure about 2 inches/ 5.5 cm from the knot and make a dot with a pen. This dot gives an indication of the length of ribbon along the inside of the egg and will be just under the top circles when the egg comes together.

7. Fold the first strip up and thread the ribbon through the two end circles. Do that with the next two strips. Thread the strips in the sequence in which they lie.

TIP: If you want to add beads to the tail, do so before starting to thread the ribbon. beads are a good way to add weight to the finished decoration.

8. Make a loose knot just above the threaded top circles after making sure that the egg has a nice shape. The dot that you you made must be under the circles and will help to determine where to make a knot. Slide the loose knot down and tighten.

TIP: To make eggs that lie in a bowl, tie a bow at both ends without a tail.
TIP: The circles can be reinforced by taping over them on the reverse side before punching holes.

CHOCOLATE WRAPPER IDEAS

TIP: Include the white edges of the book's page beyond the gingham pattern for gift wrap with a maximum size to fully wrap a large choc bar

1
A chocolate slab with the wrapper edges flattened and glued for a modern "crimped" edge look

2
Wrap the chocolate in tissue paper first, then trim the wrapper so the tissue edges show

3
The chocolate wrapper used like regular gift wrap to fully wrap the slab. See TIP

4
The full wrapper trimmed for a smaller choc

4
Make a sleeve from the wrap for a small snack choc by gluing and flattening the edges. Glue the long back seam. Glue one edge. Flatten. Insert the chocolate. Glue and flatten the other edge.

LAYER CARD INSTRUCTIONS

1. Glue numbered elements to egg and topper sheet

2. Glue backing topper to a 5x7"cardstock card
See general instructions to cut or download and print from www.anniarts.com/daffodils-clip-art

3. The finished card can be a 5x7"postcard
or fold to a 5x7" card

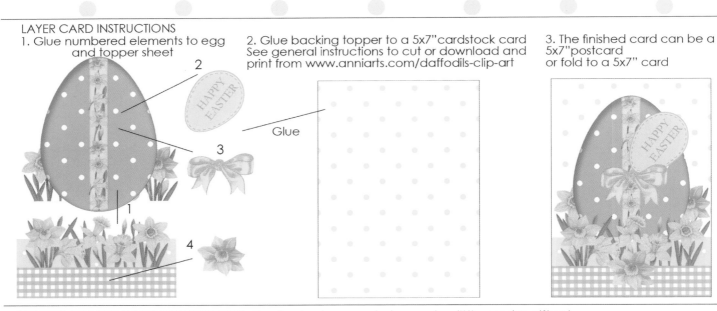

Glue

TEACUP CRADLE CARD INSTRUCTIONS. Use the teabag packet as a nice little card-n-gift set.

2 Flip card around.
The daffodil and egg is on the back of the finished card

1 Score and make a fold

Glue on under side

3 Glue top tab up to scored and folded line

Glue

4 Place back section behind front of card and line up the edges of the cup shape

Make a small cut in the rim of the cup for the egg tag

5 Optional:
Glue the teabag packet on the inside below the top tab

Put tea tag string through the cut in rim

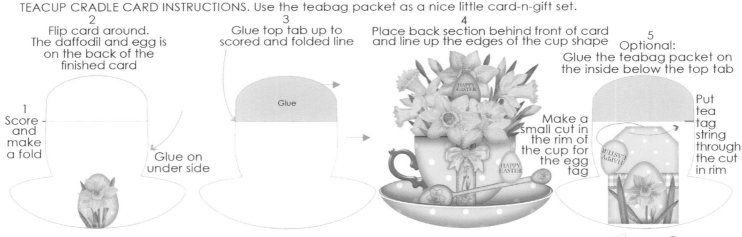

Fill the teabag packet with a teabag and replace the teabag tag with the egg tag

Printed in Great Britain
by Amazon